I0467935

CONTENTS

I dedicate this book to my dad and late mother, Jack and Ellen, and to my wife, Rica.

Mom, Dad, thank you for sacrificing your own comfort to ensure I get a proper education.

Rica, thank you for believing in me in this endeavor. It is done.

I love you guys.

INTRODUCTION

We have all heard about IQ, or Intelligence Quotient, as a way of measuring intelligence.

We have also heard about EQ, or Emotional Intelligence, as a way a person identifies different emotions in himself and in other people. Emotional Intelligence influences one's thinking and behavior.

Much has been researched, written, and said about these two factors as an indication of how successful one will become in the future.

But no one has mentioned the other piece of the puzzle which determines success.

If I may, I would like to coin the term FQ, which stands for Financial Literacy Quotient. I believe that Financial Literacy is such an important factor in determining one's success.

You may have a high IQ and EQ, but if your Financial Literacy is lacking, then you will probably end up unsuccessful when it comes to managing your finances. You may be great at your job, even a real Einstein, but when it comes to handling money, you may just be an infant.

PART ONE

STOP THE BLAME GAME

Not all college graduates are financially literate. The problem with colleges and universities, or the school system in general, is that they focus only on teaching their students how to earn money for a living. Unfortunately, they don't teach the students what to do with the money they earned, how to multiply it, and how to make their money work for them, for their future.

Academic institutions should focus not only on a child's ability to earn, but also teach a child how to manage the money he will earn in the future.

True wealth begins in the mind. Sadly, the

first few years a man earns money, he ends up practicing what he learned from his parents. He practices the same bad, or misinformed money habits which his parents have practiced all their lives.

So was it our parent's fault? To be blunt, Yes and No. Yes, because they should have educated themselves and developed their financial literacy. And No, because they also learned their wrong, or ineffective money handling methods from their parents, and so on.

When it comes to mismanaging our finances, it's easier to blame others than to admit that it was our fault. It is crucial that we accept the truth that we are one hundred percent responsible for our finances.

Change begins now, with you.

Chapter 1

Stop blaming the government

Stop blaming the government for the financial situation you're in. No matter how huge the income tax is, or how costly education, healthcare, or the cost of living are, at the end of the day, you are still responsible for your finances. Learn to accept the things you cannot control and work with the things you can control.

Let's take a look at a few examples:

- The income tax rate, you cannot control.

- Buying latte, or designer coffee, everyday, you can control.

- The cost of gasoline or diesel, you cannot control.

- The type of car you drive, you can control.

- The cost of healthcare, you cannot control.

- Buying health insurance, you can control.

- The cost of utilities, you cannot control.

- How much water and electricity you consume every month, you can control.

Bottom line:

There are a million things you cannot control. And in some ways, government policies have a lot of influence over your finances, and affect the quality of your life.

Still, when it comes to managing your finances, you are 100% in control.

After all is said and done, the only question that you should answer is this, "How well did you manage your finances?"

The government did not ask you to purchase a latte every single day.

That very expensive designer dress which you purchased using your credit card, that's on you.

That 60" plasma TV that you bought at the offer of 12 months 0% interest, so you can show off…er…invite your friends over for Super Bowl Sunday, that's also on you.

Chapter 2

Stop blaming your parents

Ok. You think your parents did not love you enough and modeled the wrong behavior and financial decisions that you picked up on. That's not it. They just did not know a better way. The good news is, you can change and unlearn these bad money habits over time.

Yes, you heard me right.

You can change your financial habits beginning today.

If you have a child or are planning to have one or two someday, please don't pass your bad money habits on to your children. Teach them not to live from paycheck to paycheck. Teach them that it's possible to have more money at the end of the month, and not vice versa, because, it is possible.

If there's a legacy you must leave to your child, first it's a proper education, so he will know how to earn money. The second is financial wisdom, so he will know what to do with the money he earns. Teach him not to love money, but to respect money. Teaching him to love money will make him greedy and selfish, thereby destroying his life in the process. Teaching him to respect money will make him responsible, able to sufficiently provide for himself and his future household.

All his decisions as an adult, will be based on this financial wisdom. It will define the quality of his life. It will equip him with the tools he would need, to be a responsible spouse and parent. And, it will make him a more responsible, productive, citizen of his country and the world.

Chapter 3

Stop blaming yourself

For lasting change to happen, you must acknowledge your mistakes, but after the acknowledgment, you must get up, dust yourself off, then move forward.

You must begin practicing good, financial choices not tomorrow, but today.

Yes you can! It doesn't matter how overwhelmingly messy your financial life is at the moment. It doesn't matter how deep your credit card debt is right now. You can change it. You can get out.

It took months and years for your debt to pile up. It might take a little longer to pay off this debt. But take heart. It is doable. It is achievable through conscious, educated, and effective money-handling decisions you will make, from this point, onward.

PART TWO

HATE BORROWING MONEY

In the Holy Bible, it is mentioned that people who borrow money, are slaves to the money lenders. Nothing can be truer than this statement.

Please note that there are two types of debt - good debt and bad debt. Good debt is what you make use of in order to prosper in life. Bad debt, is needless. It keeps you from becoming successful.

Below are a few examples of each.

A housing loan is good debt. You need to

provide a stable home for your family, and for yourself in your retirement years.

0% interest purchases on your credit card are bad debt. It's a lie. There's no such thing as an easy payment plan. Each and every payment will be difficult.

Borrowing money for an extravagant wedding is bad debt. If you really love your fiance/fiancee, please don't begin your life together buried in debt. Have a simple wedding that is within your budget. This is the only type of wedding you can genuinely be proud of. Be real and true to yourself. You don't want your first day together to be based on a lie now, would you?

Loaning money for a business is good debt, but there's an important "IF." Make sure that you have a solid business plan and that the anticipated monthly profit will be more than enough to pay off the monthly amount due on the business loan. Take a cue from the millionaires and billionaires of this world. If you're only starting out on your business, start small, not big.

Getting a car loan is good debt if the car will serve you as you travel to and from work.

Getting a car loan is bad debt if your chief motivation is to show it off to your friends or neighbors.

When in doubt, if a loan is a good debt or a bad debt, you can ask yourself the following questions:

A. What is your chief motivation for getting this loan?

B. Are you willing to give money to the bank, in the form of interest, for this loan?

C. Is it an actual need, or just a want?

If you'll just be true and honest with yourself, your spouse, and your business partners, you'll end up making the right decisions when it comes to borrowing money.

Chapter 4

Use your credit card wisely

Be a fair-weather friend to your credit card. Use it sparingly, and if you can manage, use it only for emergency situations. Emergency means anything related to healthcare. Cosmetic procedures are not covered, unless you were in some sort of an accident, or you're a model and your new nose will grossly add to your talent fee. 0% interest promos are not emergency situations. I repeat, 0% interest promos are not emergency situations.

As much as possible, purchase in cash or use a debit card. Just because everybody else is using a credit card, does not mean you have to use one as well. You're a human being, not a sheep. If you already have too much credit card debt, there's no logic in further adding to it. That's what the ATM machine is for. Believe it or not, there was a time when people did not use credit cards. Moreover, a considerable number of the world's population still do not use credit cards.

A few decades ago, the banks decided to exploit Joe, and Joanna.

The marketing and advertising companies have done their homework and they have done it well. They have transformed what were once luxury items, into necessities. They have transformed even the most illogical and mundane item, into the next big thing. Now, all the Joes and Joannas cannot sleep at night without possessing that item. Obviously, the banks wanted to cash in. They wanted their piece of the pie, so to speak. Hence, the credit card was born. And the rest, as they say, is history.

By inventing the credit card, the banks were able to use the people's basic tendency to want more and more, against them. They invented a tool that enabled people to feed off their lust for materialism. So when the credit card went in the front door, out went the virtue known as Delayed Gratification.

Note: I'm not against credit cards. I'm only against using it irresponsibly. A credit card can be a real life saver in times of emergencies. However, when it is used irresponsibly, it is detrimental to one's financial health.

Chapter 5

Love your debit card

Right now, if you have a debit card, Visa or MasterCard, you can use this for all types of purchases, even online purchases. Usually, a debit card is at the bank where an employee receives his salary. Moreover, establishments which accept credit cards will also accept debit cards, more often than not.

The nice thing about using a debit card is that you already possess the money you will use to purchase the goods. So there's no reason to feel any guilt in using it.

But make sure to set aside, or withdraw your savings first, and use the balance for your purchases.

Do this every month.

Chapter 6

Just say NO

- Say NO to overspending.

- Say NO to 0% interest offers.

- Say NO to impulse or emotional buying.

- Say YES to spending less than what you earn.

- Say YES to conscious purchasing decisions.

- Say YES to investing.

Chapter 7

Love living simply

True wealth is not your jewelry, mansion, and fancy cars. True wealth is your mindset of creating abundance. True wealth is the desire and ability to multiply what has been given to you. It's not enough that you earn a living. True wealth begins with what you do with the money that you earn. True wealth is a way of life.

A car, in many cases, is a necessity. But only you can decide if you really need one or not. If you live 15 minutes away by foot, from the office, or grocery, do you really need a car? Of course not.

I'm sure you can make a long list of why it's right to have a car, why you need a car. But, consider the alternative. Having no car offers the following benefits:

- No more gas purchases
- No more parking problems
- No more toll fees
- No more costly car maintenance
- No more car registration
- No more car insurance
- Better health (You'll be forced to walk, thereby making you more fit.)
- etc.

I'm not against owning a car. I love cars. But if you're driving a car just to show off, please reconsider. If you really need one, get one. But if not, what's the point of burdening yourself with all these responsibilities and additional expenses?

But living simply means so much more than just not owning a car. Living simply is a mindset. Living simply is a lifestyle. Living simply means being grateful for everything you have and realizing that you lack nothing.

As explained earlier, before purchasing anything, whether a car, a house, a property, watch, clothes, mobile, gadget, etc., first find out your chief motivation for buying that item. Consciously or subconsciously, you will always have a reason why you're choosing one item over another. Oftentimes, we make decisions emotionally.

Do you really need it?

Or do you want it to show off, to belong, and to be accepted?

Only you can decide.

One guideline that you can, and should follow, is to spend less than what you earn.

Chapter 8

Sleep well at night

Some people say debt is a part of life and that they cannot live without owning a credit card.

I disagree 100%. That's hogwash.

I've been living debt-free since 2010.

We paid off our mortgage last Feb 2010.

I got rid of my last credit card in 2011.

I haven't gotten a new one since.

If I need to purchase something online, I use my Visa debit card. This is where my salary gets credited.

Please don't get me wrong. I'm not saying

this to brag. From the top of my lungs, I am proudly declaring to the world that I have zero debt, and that you can live a debt-free lifestyle too.

If your culture dictates that you cannot survive without a credit card, there's something wrong. Don't let your nationality, geography, or ethnic background, dictate what you can or cannot do, what you can live or live without. As already mentioned, a significant number of the world's population does not use a credit card. Hard to believe? It's not difficult to imagine that you too can do the same.

You too can live a debt-free lifestyle!
Learn how to manage your funds. Learn how to invest. You never have to worry about receiving a foreclosure notice, or a late payment call from your bank. Ever.

PART THREE

LOVE SAVING

"Build a loving relationship with saving. Love your spouse, but make saving, and paying yourself first, your mistress."

Chapter 9

Pay yourself first

Hooray! It's the end of the month. The salary's in the bank. What do you do first?

If you were like me, when my financial literacy was still in its infancy, what I did was pay off all my bills first, then set aside my budget, my living expenses, for the next month. Then, whatever was left, I set aside, as savings.

Sounds logical, right?

This is precisely the reason why people don't do this simple process to prosperity.

This is the wrong way.

The correct way is to PAY YOURSELF FIRST.

When you come to think of it, paying yourself first is actually a misnomer. Even before you receive your salary, the company already deducted the income tax, the social security premium, the healthcare premium etc. So all you receive is the net income. So in reality, you cannot pay yourself first. But you can pay yourself second.

After all the requisite government dues, the sensible thing to do is to set aside 10% of your net income for your savings.

If you are heavily in debt, then set aside the other 20% to pay off your debt.

The remaining 70% of your income is what you use for your living expenses. Once you're finished paying off your debt, you should increase your savings to 30% per month.

Note: Savings is categorized under the following: Emergency Fund and Investment Fund. We will discuss these further in the book.

Chapter 10

Don't be a miser

Remember Ebenezer Scrooge from A Christmas Carol?

Don't be like him. He accumulated wealth for the sake of accumulating wealth. Look how it turned out for him.

Don't be a miser.

Chapter 11

Enjoy the fruits of your labor

You have to enjoy the fruits of your labor. You must enjoy the rewards of doing a hard day's work.

Not being a miser, and enjoying the fruits of your labor, are not contradictory to the notion of loving to save.

You may be just a normal entry-level employee but when it comes to your finances, you have to be a full time manager. Part of the work of managing money is balancing between consuming and saving. We can enjoy our lives and still manage to save at the end of the day.

As cliché as this may sound, it doesn't matter how much you're earning. What matters is how much you're saving. You may be surprised to know that percentage-wise, people who generally earn less, end up saving more than people who actually earn more. And as the salary increases, instead of saving more, people end up spending more and saving even less, percentage-wise, than what they used to.

Does this sound familiar?

It really doesn't make any sense but the majority of the population does this.

It boggles the mind but it's true.

I too have been guilty of committing this practice in the past.

Slowly, I've transformed my ways.

Now, I can honestly say that I am a better man because if it. The quality of my life is so much better. My finances are healthier.

Chapter 12

Build your emergency fund

Emergencies. We have all experienced emergencies at one time or another. And most of it involved money or financing of some sort.

The path to prosperity and wealth begins with preparing for emergencies. It's not a question of if it will happen, but when it will happen.

Scenario 1: Your mother called, your father was rushed to the hospital due to stomach pains he experienced. He doesn't have any health insurance since he's already retired. They need your help in settling the hospital bills and paying for medication.

Scenario 2: One Friday afternoon, on the same day you were planning to go out with your friends to celebrate a friend's promotion, your boss calls you into his office. Beside him is the HR Manager. To make a long story short, although you've contributed a lot to the company, your position was found to be redundant. Ouch! You? Of all people? You're the Mark Zuckerberg and Steve Jobs in what you do! How can they do this to you?!

The cold, hard truth is, layoffs happen all the time. No one is exempt from it. Even if you're the expert or guru in your position, your company can decide one day that they're better off hiring 2-3 good people, to do the work you're doing. In all practicality, they don't need an expert. They just need good people.

Scenario 3: The alarm clock rang. You hate it. You want to call in sick. Today. Tomorrow. And the Day After. You have lost your passion in your workplace, and in what you're doing. You want to get out. You want to do that thing which you were born to do, which your conscious and subconscious minds are pushing you to do. But you can't. You have bills to pay. The bills come like clockwork. They always do.

If you have saved up an emergency fund, then you can use it in any of these scenarios. In fact, you can use it for anything. It can be that your car needs repairing, you need to fix a leaking roof, etc.

Your emergency fund will keep you from touching your other savings, your investments.

So how big should your emergency fund be?

As a rule, your emergency fund should be big enough to cover all your expenses for 3 to 6 months, without you earning a single dime. This will depend on your lifestyle, and your situation. If you're the sole breadwinner, then it will be a considerable sum. If you're single and only responsible for yourself, then it will be a smaller amount.

No matter the amount, there's no need to rush. That's right. There's no need to rush. Your emergency fund is not meant to be completed in a short amount of time. So take your time. Just make it automatic, and make it habitual. Just 10% of your net income every month will do, or a lot more, if you can manage.

Chapter 13

Build your investments

Congratulations on completing your emergency fund! Well done.

Now, it's time to build your investment portfolio.

There are different types of investment vehicles you can choose from.

Real Estate.

Life Insurance.

Mutual Funds.

Government Bonds.

The Stock Market.

Etc.

These are the most common types. There are others such as putting up a business, or investing in gold or jewelry, investing in commodities, etc.

We will focus on the ones mentioned above.

PART FOUR

DEVELOP YOUR

FINANCIAL WISDOM

Do You Find Yourself Thinking?

"Investing is for professionals only."

"Brokers and financial advisers just want to cash in on my hard-earned money."

"I only finished high school and I'll be poor all my life, just like my parents, and my grandparents."

If yes, please stop it. Stop thinking this way.

Press Shift+Delete to remove this kind of negative thinking, permanently, from your mind.

This kind of thinking is precisely how you got yourself and your family in this difficult financial situation in the first place.

It's time to change your internal dialogue. It's time for a healthier, and more accurate mindset.

Investing is not only for the elite, or those who possess Business degrees, or those who graduated from Ivy League or top universities.

Investing is not only for the rich.

Investing is for you, your children, and your grandchildren.

Investing is for everyone.

Admit it. The only reason you refuse to talk about investing or, much less, to think about it, is right now, at this point in time, you know squat, zilch, nada!

It's time to change this. Believe it or not, there was a time when you were bold. At that time you learned and absorbed anything and everything.

If children were scared of learning, then nobody would be able to read, or write, or talk, as well as we do today.

Be a child. Be open to learning.

Real estate.
Life insurance.
Government bonds.
Mutual funds.

The stock market.

Sounds like a mouthful, don't they?

Did you know any letter from the alphabet before attending Kindergarten? No, right? You can learn all these things through books or seminars. Heck, you can even learn about these things for free, through the Internet.

Chapter 14

Read books

Read books on financial literacy and the different types of investments.

Instead of watching another hour of TV, or playing another game on your smart phone, walk or drive over to your nearest school or public library.

Everything you need to know about investing, about multiplying your money, about retiring comfortably, has already been written.

After you've read a few books which you enjoyed reading and actually understood, then please buy the books, either a physical book, or an ebook for your device. This way, the new things you've learned will be in your reach, in a moment's notice.

Never scrimp on investing on your financial education. Spend the time and money. It will be so worth it.

Chapter 15

Attend seminars

Attend seminars on Financial Literacy.

When it comes to investing, you have to be sure that the medium is right for you and that you know all the risks there are to know. The only way to do this is to congregate and converse with like-minded individuals so that you will avoid investment scams and minimize, if not completely remove, the risk of losing your hard-earned money, in the long run.

You can attend financial literacy seminars to learn different types of investments.

To illustrate, before we select a new smart phone, we check out all the specifications and features and compare these to other models and brands. We do this to ensure that the smart phone we will purchase, will be perfect for us and will satisfy all our needs for a smart phone.

What more do we need to know or do when it comes to our investments? We have to do our homework. We have to check where we want to put our money. We have to check the returns, versus the risks involved.

Warning: There is no shortage of investment scams and con artists out there. Make sure you attend seminars that are endorsed by the government and that are legal. When something is too good to be true, it probably is. One thing to keep in mind is to stay away from organizations that promise insanely high returns in a short amount of time. Most likely, these are scams and are illegal.

Chapter 16

Get financial mentors

If you want to double or triple your income in the next 5 years, or if you want to reach a certain income level like, let's say $100,000.00, you have to begin hanging out with people who have done it, and who are already earning this much.

If you want to build a successful business, you have to seek guidance from others who have started their own businesses and have thrived.

If you want to learn how to invest and make money in the stock market, you have to hang out with people who have done it, and who are doing it already.

You can get financial mentors or coaches in a variety of ways.

You can read their books.

You can sign up on their website's mailing list.

You can search for them in financial literacy seminars and build a relationship with them over time.

The wisdom of these people are invaluable. They can provide important lessons so you can avoid having to commit the same mistakes they did when they were just starting out.

Learn all that you can, then apply the lessons to your investments.

Chapter 17

Surf the Internet

Leverage the power of the Internet to your advantage. Use search engines to find the information you're looking for. Go to trusted sites and information providers.

The Internet can be used in a number of ways and developing your financial literacy is one of them.

Don't know anything about mutual funds? Search for it.

Want to know more about government bonds? Search for it.

Want to learn how the stock market works and how you can safely invest in it? Search for it.

I assure you that anything you need to know to build your financial literacy is at your fingertips. You don't even need to leave your home.

Don't have enough money or time to purchase new books or attend seminars? No problem. Just search for them on the Internet.

If you can spend 3 hours everyday slumped on your couch watching TV, you can learn about these financial investment vehicles within 15-30 minutes everyday.

You can even become an expert in your own right, by reading about these things for 15-30 minutes a day, everyday.

You can apply the old maxim for this. "If there's a will, there's a way." If you have no will, nor desire to learn these new things, then you're only left with excuses. But if you do the work, and spend your time wisely, and invest yourself in this worthwhile endeavor, then congratulations! You're on your way to financial prosperity.

PART FIVE

START INVESTING TODAY

"Failing to plan is planning to fail." -
Unknown

Now that you've completed your emergency
fund and you've paid off all your bad debts, it's
time to begin investing.

If you begin working at age 20, and will
retire at the age of 65, this gives you 45 years to
plan and prepare for your retirement. Not bad. If
you live only up to the age of 70, this means that
you'll only have 5 years to worry about and plan
for. Sounds good? Absolutely.

But, what if you live up to the age of 80, 90,

or 100? It means your total retirement years will be 15, 25 and 35 years, respectively. So it means that you have to plan and prepare for how you will support yourself for 15, 25, and 35 years after retirement. Suddenly, it sounds daunting. Suddenly, it sounds overwhelmingly impossible.

The thing that you must understand is, people are living longer and longer as the years go by. You will live longer than your parents. And your children will live longer than you.

Sure, you might not even reach the age of retirement because of your hypertension or high blood pressure, which runs in your family.

But, what if you do?

Make sure that how you manage your finances today, will provide you with the most comfortable living condition you can imagine, or it will be very difficult for you in your old age. Your old age, is the time when you should not be worrying about how to pay for your medicines, food, or utility bills.

Your retirement years are the time which you should spend with your children and grandchildren, and not become a burden to them.

Investing for your retirement is a mindset. It is a way of life. It's not a love for money but respect for money itself. It's setting aside 20-30 percent of your income every month in mutual funds, or government bonds, or buying small amounts of stocks each month, stocks from huge, gigantic corporations, that will still be there after your grandchildren have their own kids. I mean, let's face it. There are corporations that we know, instinctively, will still exist, even after we kick the bucket, pardon my French.

Sans World War III, or the Apocalypse, there are corporations that are so huge, they will outlive us, our children, and our grandchildren's children.

Investing for your retirement is not a get-rich-quick scheme. It is ensuring that you will retire comfortably in your old age. It is a constant reminder not to consume all your income every month. It is a commitment, and a promise that you're making to yourself, that you will not rely on that measly government pension, and that you will not burden your children, and their families in the future, with your cost of living. It is a hope that you will live in the most comfortable way possible, in your old age.

Chapter 18

The need for investments

Remember the old saying that the only things that are guaranteed in life are Death and Taxes? Well, this is true but not very accurate. They left out one important thing - Inflation.

When you hear people say that the inflation rate is high, they're simply saying that the cost of living rose tremendously. Rent, property, consumer goods, tuition fee, gas, cost of education, healthcare, etc. - they all rise, yearly, and no one can stop it, no superhero nor the president.

Having said this, it's important to know that when it comes to your life savings, especially for your retirement, putting it in the bank is a no-no. Your money shrinks yearly.

In a nutshell, the interest rates offered by

banks today, even time deposit rates, are not equal to the inflation rate. So the purchasing power of your $100 today, will be less a year from now. 5 years from now it will be even less. 10, 20, or 30 years from now, consider it next to nothing.

If there are two lessons I want you to learn in this entire book, it is these.

First, respect money. Don't love money. Respect money. A love for money will make you greedy and selfish and will destroy your life.

Second, you have to find a way to ensure that the growth of your money will exceed the losses brought about by inflation.

Keep your emergency fund in the bank. But keep your retirement fund (investments) in other channels where they will yield a higher return over time.

Chapter 19

Buy a home

Purchase your own home.

I cannot stress enough how important it is to purchase a home. The earlier the better.

Sure, you're still single and you don't know where life will lead you. I argue that when you're single, and have so much disposable income, that's the time when it's best to purchase a home.

At this point in your life, you're not tied to so many financial responsibilities and obligations. Instead of wasting so much disposable income, you can use it to purchase a home.

Are you planning to work abroad? Great. You can lease or rent out the property and this will earn you some passive income while you're working full time abroad. Who knows, maybe you can use this extra income to pay off the monthly amortization of your housing loan, so that in time, it will actually pay for itself.

Are you planning to migrate permanently to another country, some time in the future? Awesome. You can sell this property for much more than what you paid for it, and the money you earned will boost your finances and will assist you in the migration process.

Owning a home, or any property for that matter, is always a good, right step forward. It is a crucial step to your financial freedom. Simply put, it doesn't make sense to rent an apartment for the rest of your life. There are changes that will happen because of aging that are beyond your control.

Even if you wanted to work after the normal retirement age of 65 years, you may not be able, because your health is likely to deteriorate as you grow older.

There will come a time when you won't be able to work despite your willingness to work. My personal opinion is, nobody should have to work after they are 65 years of age.

I mean it's the twilight years of a person's life. Your time should be spent with your spouse traveling the world, or visiting places you've always wanted to visit, but didn't have the time before retiring. It's also when you should be spending more time with your family, children, grandchildren, and friends.

It also does not make sense to delay purchasing a home later in your life, when the cost of real estate is much higher. The price of real estate, like the cost of living, increases on a yearly basis. So if you're still single and have the disposable income, purchase a home. Your future self will thank your past self for being smart and starting early on your road to financial freedom.

I would say that owning a home by the time you retire, is already 75% of what you need to retire comfortably. Having a roof over your head is such an important security blanket. *But* as elementary as this may sound, people still miss out on this crucial step.

I won't question how difficult life is for a lot of people that's why they were never able to achieve or complete this important step in their lives, but for the middle class professionals, those who always had a good-paying job and never experienced being unemployed, and never had any fatal or life-threatening illness, it's sad to see them without a home once they retire.

For these people, if they decide to look back on their life, and do some genuine soul-searching, they will find that they have been irresponsible with their income. By then, it will be too late.

Chapter 20

Get life insurance

Get yourself some life insurance.

Like owning a home, I also cannot stress how important life and health insurance are.

Remember Old Age. He's there. He's waiting for you, just around the corner. And he's bringing his good buddies Sickness and Death with him.

Everybody will die, whether you care to think about it or not. No one knows when he/she will perish. I don't care what anybody else might say. Everybody should purchase some life insurance.

This is especially important if you're planning to get married and have children. Please purchase some life insurance.

The number 1 problem associated with a sudden, accidental death, is the cost involved for funeral arrangements, and state taxes on the properties and assets left by the deceased. Furthermore, with your passing, your family needs to adjust to the loss of family income.

There's a joke that the loudest funerals are for those people who don't have life insurance. The financial toll imposed on the family left behind is so much so that the members of the family end up crying, not just out of grief, but more from the real struggle of dealing with the expenses that came out of a person's demise, sudden or not.

If you're like me, after I die, I want my family - my wife, father, and siblings, to continue enjoying the fruits of my labor, namely the properties, savings, and wealth I have accumulated through my life's work.

I don't want them to have a difficult time paying for the estate tax of my home and other properties. I will ensure my wife continues to enjoy living in the house we purchased. My life insurance policy will help ensure this happens.

If you love your spouse or your children,

and you do not want them to suffer tremendously from financial expenses and losses brought about by your death, then please get some life insurance and make them your beneficiaries.

Please note that a life insurance policy is not meant to provide a windfall of cash to the family left behind. Sure, you can use it for that purpose. But in the least, it should be used to help the people left behind get back up on their feet, as painlessly and as soon as humanly possible, so they are able to adjust to life quickly after you're gone.

Chapter 21

Invest in government bonds

Government bonds are issued by a national government. There is a maturity date where the face value of the investment will be repaid. Aside from the face value, the government shall also pay interest periodically. The interest rate is guaranteed and is subject to tax. Depending on the terms of the bond, the interest will be paid quarterly, or semi-annually.

Among these three types of investments, namely government bonds, mutual funds, and the stock market, government bonds are the least risky since the government itself promises to pay the interest periodically, and the face value upon maturity. That being said, this type of investment will yield the lowest returns or interest, as guaranteed by the government.

Chapter 22

Invest in mutual funds

There are companies that pool or combine money from different investors and expertly invest for them and manage their funds. These are called mutual funds. A fund manager is the one in charge of investing the money in either bonds (or government securities,) the stock market, or a mix of these, depending on the investors' preference.

Basically, mutual funds are for people who have no time or patience to learn and invest in the stock market, money market, or government bonds. So what they do is leave it up to the fund manager to expertly manage their funds for investing. In return for his services, the fund manager/company charges a minimal fee, based on the amount of funds invested.

There are different types of mutual funds.

Depending on the country you're from, there may be more than three types of mutual funds.

In the Philippine setting, where I'm from, there are only three types.

Bond Fund - government bonds; poses the lowest risk

Equity Fund - stock market; poses the highest risk

Balanced Fund - mixed (government bonds and the stock market;) poses a medium risk

This means that if an investor chooses the Bond Fund, then the fund manager cannot invest his money in the stock market. If he chooses to put his money in the Equity Fund, then the fund manager cannot invest his money in government bonds.

The nice thing about mutual funds is that you can always add additional funds to invest in succeeding months. This is also called topping up. Usually, this is not required and is always up to the investor.

The interests earned by mutual funds are subject to tax.

Warning: Please note that interest rates and returns in mutual funds are not guaranteed. If any company or fund manager claims guaranteed returns, then be wary, it could be a scam. It is always best to check with the government to verify the legitimacy and authenticity of the company. You must also check if the fund manager, agent, or representative you're dealing with, is really authorized to do business with the company he's representing.

Chapter 23

Invest in the stock market

A few years ago, I did not know anything about the stock market. I thought it was only for financial analysts or economists. Never in my imagination did I entertain investing in the stock market.

That all changed when I read a book by Bo Sanchez, a Filipino Catholic lay preacher, who taught his maids and driver to invest in the stock market.

The concept is so simple it will blow your mind.

Through Bo Sanchez's talks and preaching, I was encouraged to invest in the stock market. Please note that there's a big difference in investing and trading in the stock market. Trading in the stock market means buying today and selling tomorrow, or after only a few hours. The moment the market price shifts, you sell immediately. While investing in the stock market means that you purchase shares of humongous, gigantic corporations every month, corporations that will outlive you, your children, and your grandchildren's children.

Regardless of the country you are from, you know instinctively that there are companies that are so stable they have been there since the time of your grandfather and you know that these companies will outlive you as well.

Every month, purchase shares from these corporations and don't cash in until your retirement. Due to market fluctuations, there will be times when you will actually see your money shrinking - that your stock portfolio actually decreased, that you actually lost money. Don't be alarmed. It doesn't matter because we're talking about long term investing. Long term investing means 10, 20, or 30 years, until you retire. I am confident that my money in the stock market will grow over time, in the long haul.

I'll let you in on a little secret. Investing in the stock market is my preferred mode of investing for my retirement. Now that I have accomplished what I need by paying off my mortgage and purchasing sufficient life insurance, I invest 10% of my income every month, buying shares of huge, gigantic corporations, in the Philippine Stock Market. I believe that this can also apply to your particular country and situation. Whether the price is up or down, just buy every month. And diversify.

"Don't put all your eggs in one basket."

Nothing can be truer than this statement when investing in the stock market. Don't just buy stocks from one company. Buy stocks from huge corporations in different fields - property, services, consumer goods, telecommunications, utilities, Information Technology, etc.

You can only purchase stocks through a stock broker. I'm fortunate because the stock broker I use offers an online portal so I am able to buy and sell shares anywhere by myself. I don't need to talk to a stock broker. I can talk to one if I want or would need to in the future.

All the companies in the Philippine Stock Market are listed on the portal. All their analysis and research are also posted for my reference. They also suggest which companies to buy, sell, or hold. The Buy Below prices are also clearly indicated to help me make the right decisions.

All buy, sell, and withdraw transactions are subject to government tax. The stock broker also charges a minimal fee on each buy, sell, or withdraw transaction. The tax and fees depend on each transaction amount.

Warning: Investing in the stock market is not a get-rich quick scheme, *and* investing in the stock market poses some real, tangible risks.

You need to study, research, and talk to a stock broker. If the risks are more than what you can stomach and handle, then you have to go with your gut instinct and choose another form of investment.

Chapter 24

Beware of investment scams

Investment scams abound. You have to be careful. I've seen people lose their entire pension and life savings to these investment scams. You have to do your homework, before you invest. If a company promises mind-blowing returns in a short amount of time, chances are, it's a scam and most likely illegal. Check with the government. Check with investment experts.

When it comes to investing your hard-earned money, don't leave anything to chance, especially if your chief motivation is missing out on an "opportunity of a lifetime." Make no mistake. There's no such thing as an opportunity of a lifetime. The only opportunity of a lifetime is winning the lottery. That's it. Investing for your retirement is not like winning the lottery. It requires informed, educated choices. It requires commitment and discipline.

CONCLUSION

The Point of Financial Literacy is not for you to love money, but for you to respect money, beginning today.

I don't care what your profession or position is. When it comes to your finances, you are the General Manager, Chief Financial Officer, and the Treasurer, all rolled into one.

You must act like these people when handling your salary, commission, or any other income.

The quality of your life during retirement, will depend mostly on how you choose to spend today.

Make no mistake. You are 100% in control and 100% accountable for each penny you earn and spend.

I know that it's your money, it's your life, and it's your choice how you will spend your hard-earned income.

But please make sure you won't regret these decisions in the future. So, start using your money wisely beginning today.

The point of it all

The point of all wealth and prosperity is to give back.

At the end of your life, your journey, you will be left with one question:

"What did you do with your life?"

Are you tired of the world you grew up in, and are still living in today?

Change begins with you.

I want you to stop living from paycheck to paycheck.

I want you to have more money left at the end of the month.

I want you to be able to support and provide all the needs of your family.

I want you to be able to donate more to your Church, more than the requisite 10% tithe.

I want you to be able to support ministries, or causes, which are dear to you.

I want you to help the abandoned elderly.

I want you to help end poverty.

I want your children to never need to feel ashamed because of what they're wearing, or because you cannot afford to buy for them the same brand of clothes or toys that their friends have.

I want you to sleep well at night knowing that tomorrow, you will not receive any calls from your bank, asking for the late payment due on your credit card, or mortgage.

I want you to feel secure in your future.

I want you to retire as comfortably as you can, without needing to wait for your measly government pension to buy your medicines.

I want you to be able to save yourself the heartache, regret, and sorrow, of having to rely on your children one day, for your living expenses. If you raised your children right, then they will help you, no questions asked. But if you managed your finances right, then they will not need to.

I want the world to be different.

I want a world where "keeping up with the Joneses" will come to mean your desire, and ability, to donate more, and contribute more to charity, than your neighbor did last month.

I want a world where the need for charitable institutions will become less and less, with the growing number of people being able to provide for all their needs, and all their family's needs.

I conclude that as more and more people become financially literate, there will be less and less inequality, and there will be more and more people wanting and needing to help society get out of the financial mess and scarcity mindset it is in right now.

I want you to wake up tomorrow, where your basic tendency to want more and more, is replaced by your need, and burning desire, to give more and more.

The question is, do you want these too? Do you want these for your life as well?

I believe, the answer is a resounding YES.

It all begins in your mind.

It all begins with Financial Literacy.

If you agree, then please share this book with your family and friends. Tweet it, post it on Facebook and otherwise share it so we can help everyone gain financial freedom. Here is the link: *http://goo.gl/BH232x*

Like my Facebook page for ongoing

inspiration and direction on your financial path to abundance:
http://www.facebook.com/RetireRich.mobi

Here are some links to other books you may find helpful:

The Total Money Makeover: Classic Edition: A Proven Plan for Financial Fitness
http://goo.gl/CzKZ84

Get a Financial Life: Personal Finance In Your Twenties and Thirties
http://goo.gl/8OO2mi

The Money Book for the Young, Fabulous & Broke
http://goo.gl/73Hqv9

How to Retire Happy, Wild, and Free: Retirement Wisdom That You Won't Get from Your Financial Advisor
http://goo.gl/7cXTPo

How to Manage Your Money When You Don't Have Any
http://goo.gl/4gzWuX

Abundance: The Future is Better Than You Think
http://goo.gl/pVhYmr

Start Late, Finish Rich: A No-Fail Plan for

Achieving Financial Freedom at Any Age
http://goo.gl/IjLgXV

Retire Young Retire Rich: How to Get Rich Quickly and Stay Rich Forever! (Rich Dad's)
http://goo.gl/q3IqjD

ABOUT THE AUTHOR

Jeffrey Sy (1976-) was born in the Philippines to a Chinese father and a Filipina mother. He moved with his wife to Dubai in 2011. He and his wife enjoys living a debt-free and credit card-free lifestyle.

He loves to write and share his views about Financial Literacy, in hopes of inspiring people to aim for and achieve a debt-free lifestyle.

He launched his website, RetireRich.mobi, in May 2014 to inspire people to manage their funds consciously and properly, so they can retire rich.

About RetireRich.mobi

RetireRich.mobi is a website dedicated to financial literacy. It is produced and updated by Jeffrey Sy, an e-Learning and WordPress Developer by profession, and a self-published author, living in Dubai, UAE. Although only in his late thirties, he wish to impart knowledge and practical wisdom to people on how to retire rich. He and his wife have been living debt-free since 2010. He also said goodbye to his last credit card in 2011, and has never looked back since.

He is a financial literacy advocate. He

believes that people are very skillful and smart when it comes to their profession, but quite short-sighted when it comes to managing their finances. He is shocked at how most people spend their income. They have such a gross disregard for their future. It's as if they will never retire one day.

"Everybody will retire one day and the earlier you prepare for it, the better it will be for you and your loved ones. Be inspired to retire rich."
- Jeffrey Sy

HELPFUL LINKS

It's one thing to read a book and another to apply the lessons you've learned in real life.

It's not easy to change money handling habits. If you're not satisfied with the way you've been taking care of your finances, you have to be committed to changing the bad, or ineffective money habits you've been practicing all your life.

I launched my website, RetireRich.mobi, in order to inspire people like you to take responsibility and be accountable for your finances. The end goal in mind is for you to retire rich.

Every week, I write an article on different steps you can take to retire rich. Please visit my website, *http://RetireRich.mobi*, and be inspired to retire rich.

========

For more about Bo Sanchez, the Filipino Catholic lay preacher and bestselling author, whom I consider my financial mentor and personal hero, please visit his website at *http://bosanchez.ph/archives/*. I guarantee that you will learn a ton about personal finance and personal growth.

You can also get a free copy of his bestselling book (in condensed version) *My Maid Invests in the Stock Market And Why You Should, Too!* by visiting *http://www.trulyrichclub.ph/* Just sign-up in his mailing list on the right sidebar, to download the ebook for free.

The online stock broker I use to invest in the Philippine Stock Market is **COL Financial**. If you'd like to learn more about them, you may visit their website at *https://www.colfinancial.com*. I enrolled in the **Easy Investment Program (EIP.)**